Acknowledgements

Illustrations by Tessa Richardson-Jones
Photographs by Zul Mukhida except for: pp. 8t Colin Skinner,
8b Tim Garrod, 9t, 24t Adam Good, 9bl, 9br Graham Horner,
16 Tim Richardson, 17br Jayne Knights, 24m Reuben Beckett,
26b Alistair Beckett, Zul Colour Library; p. 17l, 17tr
Jenny Matthews; p. 21t Johnathan Smith, Sylvia Cordaiy Photo
Library; p. 21b James Davis Photography; p. 24b Andy Purcell,
Bruce Coleman Ltd; p. 26t Mary Evans Picture Library.

The author and publisher would like to thank the staff and
pupils of Balfour Infant School, Brighton.

A CIP catalogue record for this book is available
from the British Library.

ISBN 0-7136-4154-1

First published 1995 by A & C Black (Publishers) Ltd
35 Bedford Row, London WC1R 4JH

© 1995 A & C Black (Publishers) Ltd

All rights reserved. No part of this publication may be
reproduced or used in any form or by any means – graphic,
electronic or mechanical, including photocopying, recording,
taping or information storage and retrieval systems – without
the prior permission in writing of the publishers.

Typeset in 13/20pt Univers Medium by
Rowland Phototypesetting Ltd, Bury St Edmunds, Suffolk
Printed and bound in Great Britain by
Hunter and Foulis Ltd, Edinburgh

going places

People on holiday

Barbara Taylor

Illustrations by Tessa Richardson-Jones
Photographs by Zul Mukhida

Contents

Holiday time	6
Why do people go on holiday?	8
Packing your bags	10
Holiday journeys	11
Holiday places	14
Opening a new holiday resort	18
Holiday jobs	20
Changing places	21
Choosing a holiday	22
Holidays and the environment	24
Holidays then and now	26
Index	28
Notes for parents and teachers	28
More things to do	29

A & C Black · London

Holiday time

What do you do in the school holidays? Do you go out on day trips to places such as the seaside, a theme park or the zoo? Perhaps you stay in a holiday cottage, a hotel or on a campsite?

When people are on holiday from school or work, they have time to see new places, try out new hobbies and visit friends. If you had a friend to stay with you during the holidays, where would you like to take them?

We could go rowing on the lake.

We could visit the castle.

We could take a picnic to the park.

Why do people go on holiday?

All over the world, people go on holiday for the same reasons. Some visit friends or relatives while others enjoy going on holiday to see new places and meet new people.

Some people like to go on sightseeing holidays or sporting holiday. Others enjoy going to places where the weather is hot and they can relax in the sun. Sometimes, people who have been ill go on a holiday to help them recover.

The type of holiday people choose depends on their age, their interests, their health and where they live. The cost of a holiday is also important.

Look carefully at these photographs of people on holiday in different parts of the world. Why do you think the people in the photographs have gone on holiday to these places?

(The answers are at the bottom of the next page.)

If you could go on one of these holidays, which one would you choose?

1 Tignes, France

3 Kapitas Beach, Turkey

2 Disneyland, California, USA

4 Soller, Majorca

5 Leeds and Liverpool Canal, England

Answers:

1 To ski and enjoy the beautiful scenery
2 To have fun at a themepark
3 To relax and enjoy the sunshine
4 To visit and find out about a new place
5 To enjoy the outdoors

Packing your bags

When you go on holiday, you often have to fit all your holiday things into just one bag. To help you decide which things to take, you need to think about what the weather will be like, what you will be doing and where you will be staying.

These bags have all lost their labels. Can you find the right label for each bag? Look carefully at what's inside each one.

(The answers are at the bottom of the page.)

Answers:

Bag 1 = Label 3
Bag 2 = Label 1
Bag 3 = Label 4
Bag 4 = Label 2

Holiday journeys

If you go away from home on holiday, how do you travel? Do you use more than one type of transport? How long does the journey take?

My mum took me to Scotland on the train.

We took our car on the ferry to France.

I went to America on an aeroplane.

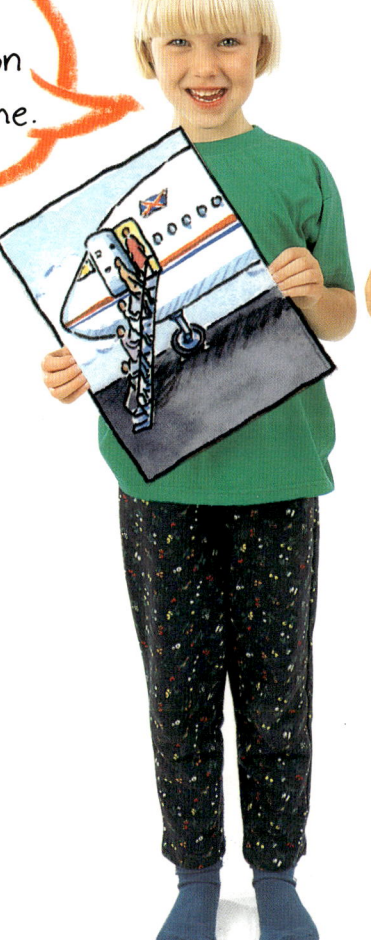

The type of transport you use depends on where you are going, how far you have to travel and how quickly you have to get there. The cost of the different types of transport may also be important.

11

If you lived in Zoltar, on the planet Kelar, you would have a choice of three different holidays:

Holiday 1 – a mountain-hopping holiday near Trag, 200km away.

Holiday 2 – a fishing holiday on the banks of Lake Spok, 350km away.

Holiday 3 – a beach holiday in Loz, 150km away.

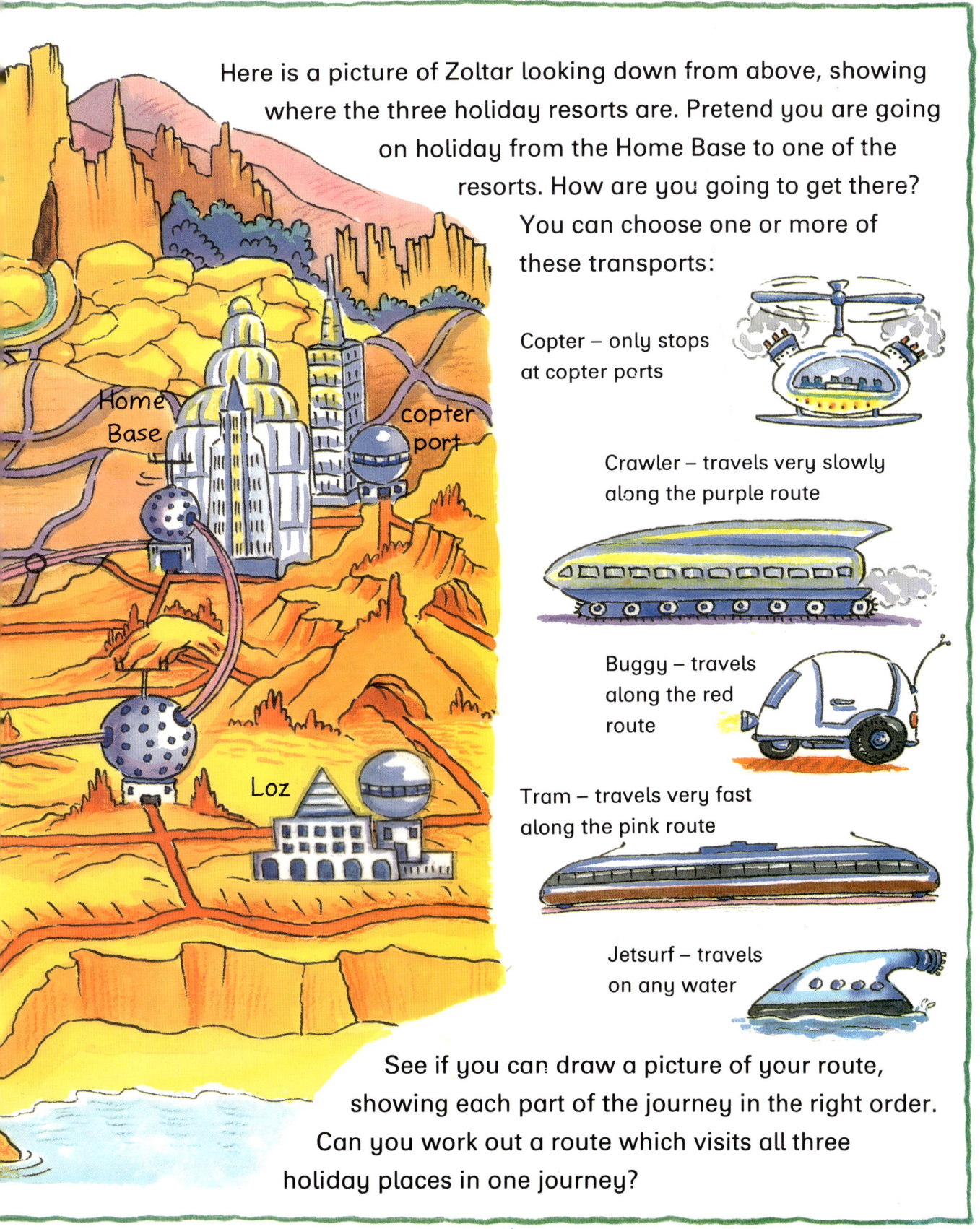

Holiday places

Some places have special features which attract a lot of holidaymakers. Many are near to the sea and have warm weather. Some have beautiful scenery or rare wildlife, and others have interesting historical features such as churches or castles.

I like to see rare animals and birds.

I like to go to places where it's warm and sunny.

I like to visit old buildings and museums.

Can you draw a map to show people what there is to see and do in your local area? You could include things like parks, playgrounds, churches, museums, beaches, woods and cinemas. You could also add useful places, such as the police station and the railway station.

Make up a simple picture for each thing you want to put on your map. Simple pictures which stand for things on maps are called symbols. Add a key at the side of the map to explain what the symbols mean.

Look carefully at these photographs of places around the world. Can you see why people go to each place on holiday? See if you can write a travel brochure entry, like this one, to point out the special features of each place. Use the pictures along the bottom of the page to help you. Which of the places would you like to visit?

Ziller Valley, Austria

If you want to get away from the crowds for your holiday and you like walking, then Ziller Valley in Austria is the place for you. Here you can enjoy lovely walks in the countryside with spectacular views and plenty of wildlife.

Features include:
* beautiful scenery
* good walking
* bikes for hire
* quiet and peaceful

museums and galleries

beautiful scenery

shops and restaurants

bikes for hire

Bangkok, Thailand

Pao de Acucar, Rio de Janeiro

Monte Carlo, Monaco

interesting old buildings

sandy beaches and water sports

good walking

quiet and peaceful

Opening a new holiday resort

Imagine you are helping to plan a new holiday resort on an island. If you were flying over the island in an aeroplane, this is what you would see.

The top of the picture is North and the bottom is South. West is to the left and East is to the right.

The island has warm, sunny weather all year round. There is only one road going from a beach to a small village in the south of the island. Rare birds nest in the forests on the slopes of the mountains in the middle of the island. The only flat land lies to the north. There are some spectacular caves at the foot of the cliffs to the east of the village. The caves can only be reached by boat.

Where is the best place to build the resort? Think about the shape of the land, the rare birds and where people live already. What buildings would your resort have and how many new roads would you need to build?

See if you can draw a map of the island. Make up symbols for all the parts of the new resort and draw them on to your map to show where everything will go. Add a key at the side of the map to explain what the symbols mean.

Holiday jobs

Would you like to work in a holiday resort? There are lots of different jobs to choose from – you might like to work as a waiter, an entertainer, a tour guide or a shop assistant.

Holiday resorts provide jobs for lots of people, especially local people. But when the holiday season ends, many people lose their jobs and have to move out of the area to look for other work.

If you were going to open a new hotel, what sort of jobs would you need to advertise? See if you can make up some job advertisements like these to put in the newspaper.

Jobs

GOLDEN SANDS HOTEL

Lots of jobs now available at the most exciting new resort to hit the south coast for years! Don't delay! Send in your application form now to beat the rush.

Tour guide

Cheerful, young, fit person needed to lead tours to nearby castles, forests and lakes. Must be able to get on well with people of all ages and stay calm in a crisis. Ability to speak at least two languages essential. Enthusiastic and outgoing personality an advantage.

Company car and travel bonus.   Ref: Z62/TFC

Lifeguard

Excellent swimmer and responsible person needed to work as a lifeguard for summer season only. Free board and lodging and use of sports facilities on site.

Send copies of swimming certificates with application.
Ref: H1/DBN

Hotel chef

Imaginative chef wanted to run busy hotel kitchen. Previous experience of tourist industry essential. Knowledge of children's menus and special diets preferred. Good salary for the right person.

Free accommodation in new luxury apartments.
Ref: E9/GLK

Children's entertainer

Could you be a clown, run a puppet show and organise a fancy dress show and a treasure hunt before lunch on your first day?

All-round entertainer urgently required to amuse children while parents relax. Huge amounts of energy and bags of ideas more important than previous experience.

Free use of all leisure facilities on site.
Ref: P54/SRP

Changing places

Look at these two photographs of Rosas, in northern Spain. One photograph was taken thirty years ago and one is a modern photograph. How has Rosas changed?

(The answers are at the bottom of the page.)

How do you think the changes affected the lives of the people who live and work there? Do you think they were pleased with the changes? Some people might think that the tourists are good for business while others might get cross with all the extra noise and traffic.

Sometimes, the huge number of people visiting a holiday resort can upset the lives of the local people. Next time you go on holiday, make sure that you respect the culture of the people you are visiting.

Rosas, 1960

Rosas, 1990

Answers:

1 The village has spread out into the surrounding countryside and there are many more houses and hotels.
2 The jetty has been extended and there are more boats.
3 The beach and seafront are much more crowded.

Choosing a holiday

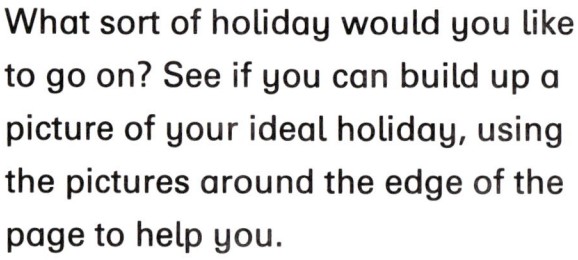

What sort of holiday would you like to go on? See if you can build up a picture of your ideal holiday, using the pictures around the edge of the page to help you.

Some people visit a travel agency to help them choose their holiday. What sort of questions would you ask a travel agent about your holiday place? Here are some ideas.

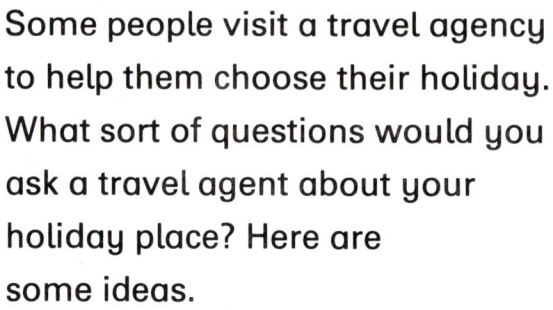

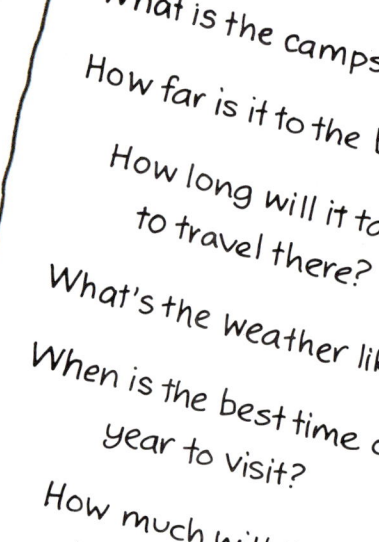

- What is the campsite like?
- How far is it to the beach?
- How long will it take to travel there?
- What's the weather like?
- When is the best time of year to visit?
- How much will the holiday cost?

Pretend you are a travel agent trying to find holidays for these people. Which is the best holiday for each group?

Eve Jones and Lucy Roberts

Ian and Lisa Williams

Jim and Meg Parker
Sam and Jo

Holiday 1

Camping holiday in beautiful French countryside. Roomy tent and all equipment provided. Swimming pool, games rooms and supermarket on site. 5 minutes drive to sandy beach.

Holiday 2

Archaeological holiday in the historic city of Templeton. Come and take part in the dig to unearth the biggest collection of Roman remains found in the last fifty years.

Bed and breakfast provided.

Holiday 3

Exciting safari adventure to the heart of the African plains. See the last great wild herds of grazing animals on Earth. Photograph a lion at 20 paces. Holidaymakers need to be fit as there's lots of walking and climbing.

23

Holidays and the environment

Holidaymakers can cause many problems for the environment.

The ferries, cars, buses and aeroplanes we use to get to and from our holidays use up lots of fuel and pollute the air.

Many towns, such as this one in Tenerife, expand to make room for more tourists, and this can destroy the natural environment.

But tourists can help to take care of the environment. For example, tourists who pay to see rare plants and animals in the wild, help to preserve the natural environment for the future.

Tourists watching the lions in Kenya. Tourists on safari like this, need to be careful they don't disturb the animals they have come to see.

What could you do to help the environment on holiday? Here are some ideas.

Holiday Code

- Take litter home or put it in a bin
- Keep to paths
- Don't make too much noise or disturb animals
- Don't buy souvenirs that you think might be made of rare plants or animals
- Don't take the beach home with you

Some people spend their holidays helping to look after nature reserves or cleaning up polluted beaches. Would you like to do that?

Holidays then and now

People only started taking holidays about one hundred years ago. Look carefully at these photographs of people on holiday at the seaside in the 1900s and the 1990s. What differences can you see?

People on the beach in Douglas, on the Isle of Man, 1905.

In 1900, only wealthy people had the time and the money to go on holiday and even then, the choice of holiday was very limited. Nowadays, cheap air travel has made it possible for many people to choose from a variety of different holidays and to visit beautiful and interesting places all over the world.

Holidaymakers sunbathing on a beach in Tenerife, in the Canary Islands.

How do you think holidays might change in the future? Perhaps people will be able to take even longer holidays. Maybe more big leisure complexes will be built where all the holiday activities are under one roof and the weather is controlled.

Computers may even be able to create a make-believe holiday in the comfort of your own home, using holograms and virtual reality headsets.

Eventually, people may be able to take holidays on other planets, such as the Moon. Would you like to go on a space holiday?

Index

Cc	campsite 6, 22
Dd	day trips 6
Ee	environment 24, 25
Hh	holiday jobs 20
	holiday season 22
	hotel 6
Jj	journey 11, 13
Kk	key 15, 19
Ll	luggage 10
Mm	map 7, 15, 19
Rr	resort 13, 18, 19, 20, 21
Ss	scenery 14, 16
	school holidays 6
	seaside 6, 14, 17, 26
	sightseeing 8
	sporting holiday 8
Tt	tourists 7, 21, 24
	transport 11, 13, 24, 26
	travel agent 22, 23
	travel brochure 16
Vv	visiting friends 8
Ww	weather 8, 10, 14, 18, 22, 26

For parents and teachers
More about the ideas in this book

Pages 6/7 Discussing play and leisure activities with children provides a good opportunity for them to talk about their lives outside school.

Pages 8/10 The reasons for taking holidays depend on factors such as wealth, work, health, leisure pursuits, weather and the location of family and friends. Some people prefer to go somewhere new on holiday; others feel more comfortable staying close to home where things are familiar.

Pages 11/13 The choice of holiday transport is influenced by the time available and the budget of the holidaymaker, as well as the landscape and climate of a particular country.

Pages 14/19 The development of places into holiday resorts is linked to features of interest, such as the history, landscape, architecture and wildlife in an area. If you live in or near a holiday resort, the children could find out about its special features.

Page 21 Tourism benefits the economy of holiday places, bringing more jobs, better roads and transport systems and more investment. But the benefits of tourism are not always felt locally. Tourism can upset local customs and job patterns, encourage crime and cause environmental problems. Tourists need to remember that they are visiting someone's home and avoid causing offence, especially when taking photos.

Pages 22/23 The most popular holiday destination is France, closely followed by the USA, Spain and Italy. One third of all tourism takes place around the shores of the Mediterranean sea.

Pages 24/25 Environmental problems caused by tourism include pollution from transport, and noise, litter and waste from holiday homes.

Pages 26/27 The increase in tourism in the last thirty or forty years is due to factors such as people having more leisure time and a better standard of living. Cheaper air travel and an increased interest in other parts of the world, have led to people taking more holidays in faraway places.

Things to do

Going places provides starting points for all kinds of cross-curricular work based on geography and the environment, looking at your locality and at the wider world. **People on holiday** explores the use of land and buildings for leisure and tourism, and looks at the impact of holidays on the landscape, transport, jobs and the environment. Here are some ideas for follow-up activities to extend the ideas further.

1 Children could visit a local railway station, bus station or an airport to find out how many of the people making journeys are going on holiday. They could make up a questionnaire to find out more about holiday travel. This could include questions such as: How long did your journey take? Did you use more than one type of transport? How far did you travel?

2 Drama activities could be developed from children taking turns to play the holiday staff and the holidaymakers, for example, a waiter serving guests at a dinner table or a receptionist welcoming people as they arrive.

3 Make a footprint-trail map which shows how to visit all the places of interest in your local area in one day. Often tourists want to see as much as possible in a short time. The children could design a clear map, perhaps with sketches or photographs of the things to see around the edge. Are there any facilities for disabled holidaymakers? The children could also make up a timetable to show how much time should be spent at each place.

4 Investigate the history of tourism and look at how it has changed since the 1960s. Facts and figures collected could provide the basis for maths activities on handling data such as holiday places most frequently visited, methods of holiday transport and numbers of people working in the tourist industry.

5 Find out about holidays in the past. At the beginning of the century, there were no package holidays abroad and most people went to British seaside resorts for their holidays. The children could find out about seaside entertainments, such as a Punch and Judy show, a pierrot show, donkey rides and slot machines.

6 The children could design and build a model of their ideal holiday resort. This would provide an opportunity for them to discuss their likes and dislikes. The children could also draw a pictorial map of their ideal resort to use in an advertisement for the opening. How many new jobs would the resort create?

7 Children could make a book of postcards and holiday brochures of the places they have visited on holiday. They could take turns being a travel agent trying to sell the holidays.

8 Ask the children to write postcards home from a place they would like to go on holiday. What sort of things would they write about? There is not much space on a postcard so the writing needs to be clear and concise.

9 Choose a worker in a holiday resort and draw a cartoon strip of a 'day in the life of' this worker. Would the children like to work in a tourist resort when they leave school?

10 Encourage the children to find out more about how holidaymakers can disturb or destroy wildlife habitats. For example, animals such as turtles, seals and seabirds can be driven off the beaches where they nest and raise their young. In some resorts, part of the beach is fenced off to protect wildlife. Is this a good idea? Also, the huge number of souvenirs made from parts of animals, such as shells, coral and skins, have reduced the number of animals actually living in tourist areas.

11 Make a calendar of jobs throughout the year in a holiday place. How do the jobs change in the tourist season? What happens to all the workers when the tourists leave? Do local people work in the tourist industry, or do workers come in from outside the area?